CREEPY CRAWLIES

Scurrying Cockroaches

Jon Eben Field

Crabtree Publishing Company

www.crabtreebooks.com

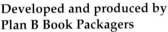

Developed and produced by
Plan B Book Packagers

Author:
Jon Eben Field

Editorial director:
Ellen Rodger

Art director:
Rosie Gowsell-Pattison

Logo design:
Margaret Amy Salter

Editor:
Molly Aloian

Proofreader:
Crystal Sikkens

Project manager:
Kathy Middleton

Production coordinator
& prepress technician:
Katherine Berti

Photographs:
Istockphoto: Intergalactic Design Studio: p. 5 (top); Saga Yago:
    p. 10 (top); Todd Media: p. 21 (bottom right)
Photos.com: cover, logo
Public Health Image Library (PHIL) of the Center of Disease
    Control: p. 16 (bottom)
Shutterstock: cover, p. 1–2; Aaron Amat: p. 6 (bottom left); Arkady:
    p. 24 (bottom right); Yuri Arcurs: p. 22 (bottom); Chichinkin:
    p. 11 (top); Paul Cowan: p. 25 (bottom); Vladimir V. Georgievskiy:
    p. 23; Glue Stock: p. 4 (bottom); Joe Gough: p. 6 (top); Mau Horng:
    p. 3, 13 (top), 15 (top), 19 (bottom), 20 (bottom); Lucio Tamino
    Hollander Correia: p. 4 (top); Pawel Kielpinski: p. 8, 15 (middle);
    Knorre: p. 12 (top); K.L. Kohn: p. 11 (bottom); Vadim Kozlovsky:
    p. 19 (top); Kushch Dmitry: p. 12 (bottom); Levent Konuk: p. 7;
    Katarzyna Mazurowska: p. 20 (top); Pensive Dragon: p. 18;
    Barbara J. Petrick: p. 15 (bottom); Pling: p. 29 (bottom); Ivelin
    Radkov: p. 14; Velin Radkov: p. 6 (bottom right), 21 (bottom left);
    Chuck Rausin: p. 26; Dr. Morley Read: p. 9 (bottom), 16 (top),
    25 (top); S1001: p. 24 (left); Sergey Toronto: p. 21 (top), 27,
    28 (top); Ljupco Smokovski: p. 29 (top left); Robert Paul Van
    Beets: p. 5 (bottom); Vatikaki: p. 9 (top); Connie Wade: p. 22 (top);
    Alaettin Yildirim: p. 10 (bottom); Lisa F. Young: p. 29 (top right);
    Dusan Zidar: p. 28 (bottom); Yakovleva Zinaida Vasilevna:
    p. 13 (bottom)

Library and Archives Canada Cataloguing in Publication

Field, Jon Eben, 1975-
    Scurrying cockroaches / Jon Eben Field.

(Creepy crawlies)
Includes index.
ISBN 978-0-7787-2502-2 (bound).--ISBN 978-0-7787-2509-1 (pbk.)

    1. Cockroaches--Juvenile literature. 2. Cockroaches as carriers of
disease--Juvenile literature. I. Title. II. Series: Creepy crawlies (St.
Catharines, Ont)

QL505.5.F53 2010   j595.7'28   C2010-901979-2

Library of Congress Cataloging-in-Publication Data

Field, Jon Eben.
  Scurrying cockroaches / Jon Eben Field.
      p. cm. -- (Creepy crawlies)
  Includes index.
  ISBN 978-0-7787-2509-1 (pbk. : alk. paper) -- ISBN 978-0-7787-2502-2
(reinforced library binding : alk. paper)
  1. Cockroaches--Juvenile literature. I. Title. II. Series.

  QL505.5.F54 2011
  595.7'28--dc22
                                                    2010011286

Crabtree Publishing Company

www.crabtreebooks.com   1-800-387-7650

Printed in China/072010/AP20100226

Published in Canada
Crabtree Publishing
616 Welland Ave.
St. Catharines, Ontario
L2M 5V6

Published in the United States
Crabtree Publishing
PMB 59051
350 Fifth Avenue, 59th Floor
New York, New York 10118

Published in the United Kingdom
Crabtree Publishing
Maritime House
Basin Road North, Hove
BN41 1WR

Published in Australia
Crabtree Publishing
386 Mt. Alexander Rd.
Ascot Vale (Melbourne)
VIC 3032

Contents

Skitter Scatter

Late at night and hungry for a snack, you walk into the kitchen and turn on the lights. Whoa! What are all those fast-moving bugs? Where did they go? Most likely, they were cockroaches. One of the most hated and feared insects, cockroaches love to live with humans and have done so for centuries.

Eeek!

Most people really don't like cockroaches. Cockroaches are seen as dirty, disease-carrying, nearly **indestructible** insects. Even though cockroaches spend a great deal of time cleaning their bodies, they spread disease because they feed on rotten food and garbage. Killing cockroaches is not easy. Cockroaches can survive extreme physical punishment due to the flexible construction of their disk-shaped bodies. If that is not enough, cockroaches also smell bad. They have a thin layer of skin over their **exoskeleton** that produces a stinky liquid that is discharged when they are scared.

Bug scientists believe that cockroach species **skittering across your bathroom floor will outlive the human race because of their ability to adapt to different living conditions.**

Cockroaches can sometimes be smelled before they are seen.

4

They're Taking Over!

Cockroaches have a remarkable ability to reproduce in great numbers. One female German cockroach can lay between 300 and 400 eggs during her lifespan of one year. Since it takes 40-45 days for a cockroach to mature, two cockroaches can create an **infestation** very quickly.

Two mature cockroaches could soon mean an infestation.

The Big Apple's Big Problem

New York City is home to a very large population of cockroaches. In fact, there are so many cockroaches and other creepy crawlies that the police department has a full-time **entomologist**. By studying the insects on a dead body, this scientist can help determine the time of death. Many big cities have public health departments and public health entomologists to study pests such as cockroaches and help develop ways to limit infestations. Limiting infestations cuts down on the diseases spread by the creepy crawlies.

New York is home to a lot of people and a lot of pests that inhabit apartment buildings and other living and working spaces.

THAT'S CREEPY

Creepy Stuff

Cockroaches are omnivorous **scavengers**, which means they will eat almost anything. Rotten meat, belt leather, paper, dead skin (either on or off humans), their own **feces**, hair, pet food, cheese, dirty clothing, grease, and glue are just some of the things cockroaches are known to chomp on. One study found that twelve cockroaches can live for one week eating just the glue from one postage stamp!

Bright Light, Big Scatter

Cockroaches do not like light. Many people don't realize that they have cockroaches living in their homes because roaches hide during the day. They emerge at night to look for food and water. They like kitchens, bathrooms, and sewers. Cockroaches can survive on just about any food and very little water. Also, because their bodies are so small and flexible, they can very easily squeeze into nooks, crannies, and crevices when threatened.

Roaches can climb up through drains at night.

Cockroaches will eat whatever they can find. An unattended bowl of dog food or glue is as good as a slice of fresh bread.

Is it Contagious?

Cockroaches can spread diseases to humans. One study found that cockroaches carry close to 50 different types of pathogens, or **microorganisms** that can cause disease. The main way cockroaches transmit disease is through contact with humans or food. Food safety inspectors keep an eye out for cockroaches at restaurants because of this danger. Cockroaches can also make life miserable for **asthma** and allergy sufferers. Once a cockroach reaches a certain size, it splits its skin and leaves it behind. This process is called molting. The skin molts, or exuvia, are thought to increase allergies and worsen asthma.

Asthma can worsen and make an inhaler necessary when there is a cockroach infestation.

THAT'S CREEPY

Headless Roach

As creepy as it sounds, cockroaches are capable of living without their heads. Since cockroaches do not have a highly pressurized **circulatory system** (like blood in our **cardiovascular system**), once the head is gone and the wound is sealed, life continues for the cockroach. Unlike humans, cockroaches breathe through small holes called spiracles located throughout their bodies, so they don't need their heads to breathe. Also, because roaches can survive for weeks without eating, losing their mouths is not a problem.

Cockroaches have been living on Earth virtually unchanged for 300 million years. Modern humans have only existed for 200,000 years. Roaches are true survivors!

Cockroach Fossils

Fossils of prehistoric cockroaches appear in the Cretaceous period (145 to 65 million years ago). Cockroach fossils are often found preserved in **amber**. When trees in prehistoric times received a shock, they produced a **resinous** sap that trapped insects. This sap hardened and preserved the insects. On many samples, the insect's original colors, veins in the wings, and eye structure are clear and visible.

Roaches have changed very little in 300 million years.

Town and Country Roach

Pest cockroaches have lived near humans for a long time. Our early **ancestors'** hunting patterns and lifestyle made them very attractive to roaches. Humans always produce garbage, always need water, and always need warmth. Cockroaches could always be sure of a meal around humans. But there are only about 20 species of cockroaches that live in human environments. The rest are wild cockroaches. Wild cockroaches live outdoors in a variety of **habitats**. Humans are also largely responsible for introducing cockroach species to new territories. Cockroaches were early hitchhikers, more than happy to come along with humans for the ride and adapt to wherever they were dropped off.

Scientific Study

Like many insects, cockroaches have suffered from a human-centered view of the world. Human dislike and fear of cockroaches prevented the insects from being seriously studied until the mid-1900s. Even now, many professional cockroach researchers rely on funding from pest control companies, whose aim is to eliminate or control the insect.

Wild roaches and pest roaches have different habitats. Some of the research done on cockroaches today is funded by the pest control industry.

Ever wonder how the world is organized? **Biologists** have spent centuries figuring out how different living things are related to one another. An ecosystem is a biological map of the relationships between the species of plants, animals, bacteria, and fungi in an environment.

Classifying Life-forms

The scientific classification, or grouping, of animals is a tool used by biologists to understand relationships between species. Biologists organize the natural world into categories and subcategories to show how animals, plants, **invertebrates**, and other living things have **evolved**. The classification system is organized by kingdom, phylum, class, and order. There are also subcategories such as family. All of the subcategories divide living things into smaller and smaller closely related groups that share common **ancestry** or characteristics.

Carl Linnaeus was a Swedish scientist who developed the system of classifying life-forms in modern biology. This system, called taxonomy, uses Latin names to identify animals and plants.

Animal, Vegetable, Insect?

Cockroaches belong to the Animalia kingdom. Within this kingdom, they belong to the Arthropoda phylum, which literally means many-jointed legs. Cockroaches belong to the Insecta class. Of the nearly one million species in the Animalia kingdom, close to 800,000 species belong to the Insecta class. That means that 80 percent of all animals are insects! Cockroaches belong to the Blattaria order which contains five main cockroach families.

Roach Families

There are around 4,000 known cockroach species, yet extensive scientific study has been limited to a very small number of species. The cockroach families are: Blattidae, with around 600 species and Blaberidae, which has around 1,000 species. The Blattellidae family has over 1,750 species, while the Polyphagidae and Cryptocercidae families have four species.

Madagascar hissing cockroaches are the largest species of cockroaches. They are wingless and belong to the Blaberidae family.

This discoid roach is a tropical species from Mexico, and Central and South America.

A Roach For All

There are so many cool cockroach species that it is difficult to separate them from the pests who crawl up our drain pipes.

A Few Pests Spoil the Bunch

The common pest cockroaches in North America are the German cockroach (*Blattella germanica*), the oriental cockroach (*Blatta orientalis*), the Australian cockroach (*Periplaneta australasiae*), and the American cockroach (*Periplaneta americana*). Each of these cockroaches is a distinct species. A species is a group of animals that is **genetically** similar and capable of reproducing both male and female young.

Native Species

Don't let the names fool you. The German and Australian cockroaches **originated** in Asia, while the American cockroach is thought to have originated in Africa. But cockroach pest species are only a tiny part of the cockroach family. Consisting of five separate families, there are almost 4,000 cockroach species. Many of these cockroaches are **indigenous** to tropical areas, but even the United States has around 60 native cockroach species.

The German cockroach is one of the most common household species. These creepy pests love sugar, grease, and meats but will eat toothpaste if they can get at it.

The roach is at home even in a tropical paradise.

The Germans

German cockroaches are small—between 0.5 to 0.6 inches (1.3–1.5 cm) in length. They thrive in human habitats. They love eating starch such as bread or pasta, grease, and meat, but also survive on glue and their own droppings. They have also been known to resort to **cannibalism** in times of scarce food. With their ability to squeeze their small bodies into tiny cracks and crevices, they are difficult to **exterminate**. Even though the German roach has wings, it cannot fly.

The Americans

American cockroaches are one of the most common cockroaches and are also known as waterbugs or palmetto bugs. This large cockroach is about 1.6 inches (4 cm) in length and is incredibly fast. The American cockroach set a world record by traveling 3.4 mph (5.5 KPH). For humans, this would mean running at 205 mph (329 KPH). If you could run this fast for 14 hours, you could travel from New York City to San Francisco. That's one fast cockroach!

The American cockroach is a fast mover.

Life Cycle

In conditions with proper food, water, and warmth, cockroaches reproduce and grow very quickly. **Pheromones** play a large role in the adult **reproductive cycle**. Female cockroaches like calm atmospheres when mating. Male cockroaches that give off a laid-back, non-aggressive smell are the ones who are successful in mating.

Ootheca

Once cockroaches have mated, the female of most species creates an ootheca. This strong egg case surrounds and protects the cockroach eggs from danger. Although a few species leave their egg cases to fend for themselves, the majority of species carry the case partially attached to the adult female's abdomen. This strategy means that it is very hard to get rid of a cockroach population once they are established. Depending on the species, egg cases can contain from four to 40 eggs. Once the eggs are ready, the ootheca is dropped.

Many female cockroaches only mate once in their life. After mating, they are pregnant for the rest of their lives.

This image shows a female German cockroach with an ootheca.

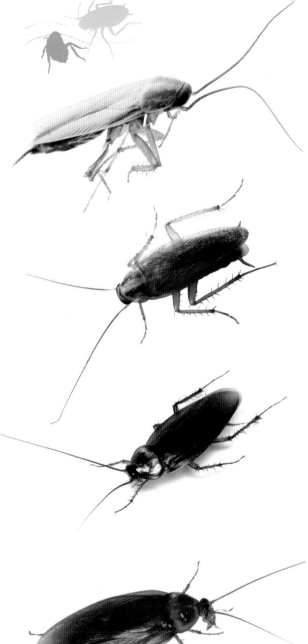

The Germans

German cockroaches are small–between 0.5 to 0.6 inches (1.3–1.5 cm) in length. They thrive in human habitats. They love eating starch such as bread or pasta, grease, and meat, but also survive on glue and their own droppings. They have also been known to resort to **cannibalism** in times of scarce food. With their ability to squeeze their small bodies into tiny cracks and crevices, they are difficult to **exterminate**. Even though the German roach has wings, it cannot fly.

The Americans

American cockroaches are one of the most common cockroaches and are also known as waterbugs or palmetto bugs. This large cockroach is about 1.6 inches (4 cm) in length and is incredibly fast. The American cockroach set a world record by traveling 3.4 mph (5.5 KPH). For humans, this would mean running at 205 mph (329 KPH). If you could run this fast for 14 hours, you could travel from New York City to San Francisco. That's one fast cockroach!

The American cockroach is a fast mover.

Anatomy Lesson

A cockroach exoskeleton is made up of a hard substance called chitin. Their bodies are strong and flexible, allowing them to withstand the force of a stomping foot, as well as squeeze into tiny crevices. Cockroaches breathe through tiny holes called spiracles located throughout their bodies. Spiracles are connected to special tubes called tracheae that distribute air to the cockroach's cells. So a cockroach doesn't need its mouth to breathe!

A cockroach's mouth has strong biting and crushing jaws with teeth called mandibles.

A cockroach's head has a long set of antennae that originate on either side of a set of compound eyes.

A cockroach's compound eyes have a large number of lenses that provide a wide field of vision. They are not able to see objects as clearly and detailed as humans.

Cockroaches belong to the superorder Dictyoptera which means having two sets of wings.

Cockroaches process their food in the gut located in their abdomen.

All cockroaches have six jointed legs covered with small bristles. These sensitive hair-like parts of the leg allow cockroaches to sense minor changes in the environment around them.

Cockroach legs also have tiny pads near their end that allow them to climb virtually any surface, even glass.

A Head For Business

A cockroach antenna is designed to sense the environment. Each antenna has 356 segments, but scientists don't understand what the majority of these segments sense. Cockroach eyes also allow them to react very quickly to danger. Mandibles help cockroaches bite and chew. A smaller set of jaws, called maxillae, are important in maintaining the cleanliness of a cockroach's mouth and antennae. Cockroaches also have extremely sensitive ears for detecting vibrations.

Flying Roaches...Ick!

The first set of wings on a cockroach are hard and leathery. These cover the more fragile flying wings underneath. Although most cockroaches have wings, not all species are able to fly. Some, such as the large Madagascar hissing cockroach, do not have wings at all. Most pest species are poor fliers as a result of living as scavengers for long periods of time. Most wild cockroaches have kept their ability to fly.

Cockroach "Pepper"

Cockroaches process their food in the gut located in their abdomen. Cockroaches also expel a pepper-like poop from their abdomens. Some cockroach experts say that an infestation can be judged by the amount of "pepper" scattered near where roaches eat and rest.

Life Cycle

In conditions with proper food, water, and warmth, cockroaches reproduce and grow very quickly. **Pheromones** play a large role in the adult **reproductive cycle**. Female cockroaches like calm atmospheres when mating. Male cockroaches that give off a laid-back, non-aggressive smell are the ones who are successful in mating.

Ootheca

Once cockroaches have mated, the female of most species creates an ootheca. This strong egg case surrounds and protects the cockroach eggs from danger. Although a few species leave their egg cases to fend for themselves, the majority of species carry the case partially attached to the adult female's abdomen. This strategy means that it is very hard to get rid of a cockroach population once they are established. Depending on the species, egg cases can contain from four to 40 eggs. Once the eggs are ready, the ootheca is dropped.

Many female cockroaches only mate once in their life. After mating, they are pregnant for the rest of their lives.

This image shows a female German cockroach with an ootheca.

From Ootheca to Adult

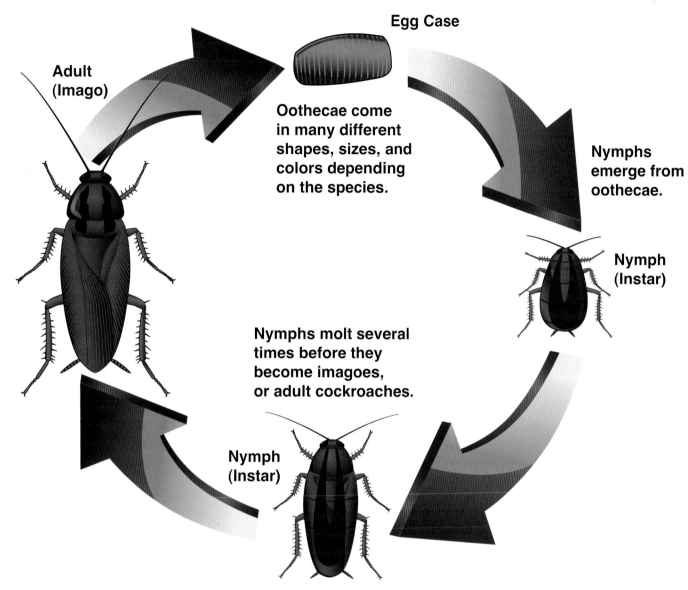

Egg Case

Oothecae come in many different shapes, sizes, and colors depending on the species.

Adult (Imago)

Nymphs emerge from oothecae.

Nymph (Instar)

Nymphs molt several times before they become imagoes, or adult cockroaches.

Nymph (Instar)

Nymphs, Instars, and Imagos

Once a cockroach hatches from its egg it is known as a nymph. A nymph molts, or sheds, its exoskeleton four to 14 times as it grows into an adult. In between each molt, the nymph is known as an instar. The instar stage is when the new, bigger exoskeleton hardens. When a cockroach nymph reaches its last instar molt, it becomes an imago. This is its final adult form. The life cycles of different species vary from three or four months to over a year to reach adulthood. Other factors that affect the life cycle are a lack food, water, or warmth.

17

Roach Habitat

Pest cockroaches like human dwellings because of the easy access to food, water, and warmth. Cockroaches love apartment buildings, restaurants, and hospitals. Cockroaches also use heating ducts and spaces behind walls as hideouts or as roads to move around undetected in these buildings and complexes.

Warm and Inviting

Almost all pest cockroaches are tropical species and they prefer temperatures of 80°F (27°C) or above. Cockroaches also like it dark and moist. They thrive in basements, sewers, kitchens, bathrooms, garbage chutes, water pipes, greenhouses, pantries, as well as behind cupboards and under subfloors. Most cockroaches are nocturnal, meaning they hide out during the day and emerge at night to scrounge for food and water.

Your house is their habitat, as long as it is warm, dark, and moist at least some of the time.

In the Wild

Most wild roaches live in dead leaves and soil on the floors of temperate or tropical forests. There, they play an important role in the decomposition of leaves by eating them, and leaving their feces as fertilizer to enrich the soil. Some species eat rotting wood. Wild cockroaches also come in a wide range of colors including green, red, blue, and dull yellow.

Wild roaches eat decaying forest matter.

CRAWLY FACT

Make Yourself At Home

Why, certainly, Mr. and Mrs. Cockroach, we'd love for your family to move into our home! On second thought, maybe not! Cockroaches are almost always uninvited guests. But how do they get into a building in the first place? A very common way is through food that has been contaminated with cockroach eggs. If the eggs come in, then there will be cockroaches. As well, many adult cockroaches are attracted to garbage. They have a strong sense of smell, and they find small cracks in foundations, walls, or an open window to squeeze themselves inside. They can also move through sewers and enter a building through drains. Once inside, they disappear into the walls during the day and eat garbage, compost, or other food at night.

Infestation

Cockroaches on the kitchen floor in the middle of the day? If you see cockroaches during the day in your home, your home is likely infested.

One or One Hundred?

Pest control experts have a rule: "When you see one cockroach during the day, there are 100 that you do not see." An infestation occurs when a very large number of cockroaches are living, eating, and breeding in a human dwelling.

Getting Rid of Roaches

The most effective way to eliminate cockroaches is to get rid of food and water sources. Clear cupboards of old or rotting food. Empty the garbage every day. Do not leave pots in the sink. Make sure drains are clean and that pipes do not leak.

A sink full of dirty dishes is like a buffet for cockroaches. All they have to do is crawl up and dig in.

Cockroaches are masters at hide and seek. It is a safe bet this guy has a few friends he hangs out with.

Roach traps are one way to kill the pests.

Traps and Sprays

Roach traps attract roaches with a scent, then the insects become trapped in either a cage or on sticky paper. Roach sprays and bait are other methods of killing roaches. The bait attracts the roach and it eats a quantity of what is actually a slow-acting poison. This roach will return to the nest and die. Other roaches consume the poisoned body, spreading the poison throughout the community. Cockroach traps and roach bait are effective with small infestations, but large ones require professionals.

The Professionals

The pest control industry is big business. Pest control experts, called exterminators, generally use powerful chemicals that eliminate all life-forms in an area. These chemicals are often toxic and require people to leave their homes for several days. Afterward, any exposed surfaces have to be regularly cleaned to prevent people from becoming ill from the harsh chemicals.

pets or Pests?

Cockroach fanciers are people who love to keep roaches as pets. Fanciers often choose **exotic** species to keep as pets. Some choose large or brightly colored roaches, while others choose roaches with strange behaviors.

A Pest Store?

Cockroaches can be ordered through insect dealers on the Internet. The most common species sold are the Madagascar hissing cockroach, the lobster cockroach, the Turkistan cockroach, the Surinam cockroach, and the death's head cockroach. Many pet stores will also have cockroaches for sale because they are used as food for other pets like lizards, snakes, turtles, and frogs.

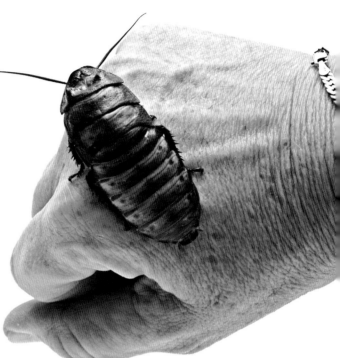

Imagine how creepy it would be to let your pet roach crawl all over you?

Although many people keep cockroaches for pets, others breed cockroaches to feed their lizards, snakes, and amphibians.

22

Madagascar hissing cockroaches, known as hissers, hiss by forcing air through their spiracles.

Home Sweet Home

Aquariums make ideal enclosures for house pet cockroaches. Bedding consists of wood shavings for species that live on forest floors or peat soil for species that live underground. Egg cartons make ideal ground coverings as they provide plenty of dark spaces to hide. Most roaches survive well on a high protein diet of cat food or roach food. Water is important, and needs regular changing. Once or twice a week, a small amount of fruit or vegetable is ideal, but needs to be prevented from spoiling. Cockroaches need a warm aquarium for breeding. Most cockroaches can climb slick surfaces like glass, so a thin layer of Vaseline is recommended at the top of the aquarium to prevent escapees. A tight, secure cover with a fine mesh to allow airflow is essential for most species.

Predators and Prey

Cockroaches are omnivorous scavengers, so they don't have any actual prey. They only eat dead things. But cockroaches are prey for a great number of **predators** and host to a number of **parasites**. Many animals from birds to frogs to cats think cockroaches are a tasty, crunchy snack.

Wild About Roaches

In the wild, cockroaches serve as a source of protein for many tropical animals. Cockroach predators range from birds to snakes to lizards to frogs to mice and other rodents. Although spiders and scorpions enjoy cockroaches, they are not useful for controlling roach populations. Some wasp species are predators on the oothecae, while others feed on both adult cockroaches and nymphs. Millipedes are quite effective at killing cockroaches, but are not welcome household guests either. In the wild, cockroach populations are kept in check. In human environments, predators are less present, although some house cats are reported to nibble on cockroaches.

Scorpions eat cockroaches but you wouldn't want to fill your house with them. Some house cats will chomp on roaches but are unlikely to help with an infestation.

It Takes an Army...

Army ants are an African ant species. They form a long column of raiding insects and prey on any living thing they encounter. These ants can be slightly dangerous to sick and old people, but their primary prey is other insects. Army ants love pest cockroaches. A column of army ants will strip a house of cockroach adults, nymphs, and eggs. Columns of army ants will gather six or seven feet high (1.8–2.1 meters) and pull cockroaches off ceilings in homes if that is where the cockroaches try to hide.

Army ants will launch raids on homes where cockroaches live.

CRAWLY FACT

Nature's Janitors

Cockroaches are great at recycling waste. Whether in a forest or in an apartment, cockroaches scavenge for dead and decaying material. When they eat, their digestive tract transforms that material into **fertile** droppings. Cockroaches eat enormous amounts of trash. Without cockroaches, both the pests and the wild ones, the world would have a lot more garbage.

Cockroaches eat decaying plant matter on a forest floor.

La Cucaracha

Humans have long been frustrated and fascinated by cockroaches. They appear as characters in books, music, and movies. Sometimes cockroaches are seen in a sympathetic light, and sometimes they are viewed as villains.

ROACH IN SONG

During the Mexican revolution of 1910, an old Spanish folk song called "La Cucaracha," or "The Cockroach," became popular. There are many versions of the song. In some versions, the lyrics support the revolution while others support the then harsh government. Lyrics were often made up to fit specific occasions and events, but the music and melody are always the same.

MAN TO ROACH

One of the most famous short stories in literature is about a man who transforms into a cockroach. Franz Kafka's book *Metamorphosis* begins with its lead character, Gregor Samsa, waking up as a cockroach. Gregor is treated poorly and abandoned by his family because of his cockroach appearance.

"La Cucaracha" is often performed by Mexican singers and guitarists.

WORDS OF HATE

Cockroaches are associated with filth and garbage, so most people have a negative reaction to them and want to get rid of them. The word cockroach has been used as a term of hate or to express contempt for people. In the 1994 mass killings in Rwanda, Africa, known as the **Rwandan genocide**, those who encouraged the killings often called those who were killed cockroaches. They did this to make their hateful actions seem less appalling. During the **Holocaust**, Nazi **propaganda** associated the Jewish people with cockroaches to make their victims appear less human.

ROACH PAL

In the film, Wall-E, a cockroach is the only living creature on planet Earth. Wall-E's cockroach friend follows him around while the robot tries to clean up the environmental devastation of Earth.

ROACH WRITER

A fictional cockroach named archy is the author of one of the most famous cartoon strips of the early 1900s. The cartoons were written by archy jumping on writer Don Marquis' typewriter keys. As archy could not hold down the shift key and a letter, all of the strips are written in lower case, and so is archy's name.

A modern archy would use a computer keyboard.

27

Crazy Critters!

Cockroaches are awe-inspiring insects. They are messy roommates that are hard to get rid of and can adapt to many situations. Would cockroaches survive a nuclear reaction? Possibly. Will cockroaches lay eggs in a human's ear? Not likely. There are plenty of things to learn about these amazing pests.

Cockroaches can handle 12 to 15 times the **radiation** a human being can endure because of their tough exoskeletons. Humans die at an exposure of 800 rems of radiation. Cockroaches die after exposures between 67,500 to 100,000 rems. Cockroaches just might be able to survive a nuclear blast that would surely kill humans.

In 2001, Ken Edwards recorded the Guiness Book of World Record's highest number of cockroaches eaten in a minute. How many? 36. Eww!!

Experts don't recommend squishing a roach under your foot. Even if you kill the adult, it could be a female and the force of your foot can break open the egg case. Once the eggs hatch, you have accidentally added to the cockroach population.

Some people think that a house or building has to be dirty to have cockroaches. This is not true. Cockroaches will live in any environment that supplies their needs, whether that is clean or dirty.

Yale University in Connecticut had a cockroach problem in one of its libraries that it dealt with in an interesting way. Along with other insects, the cockroaches were eating the paper and binding glue of the books. The university decided to rid itself of the insects by cutting heat to the library for several days in the winter and freezing them to death.

Although not drunk for its taste, cockroach tea is a folk medicine cure for dropsy, a swelling of tissue also called edema. Cockroaches fried in oil are also served up as a cure for indigestion.

Pest Detective

Knowing what a cockroach likes and needs will help you find them. Two students in New York City caught 200 roaches in a supermarket. Even more incredible is that one of their roaches turned out to be a new species. Check out the following resources to find out more about what insect entomologists call nearly perfect adapters.

WEB SITES

Here are some cool sites to check out:

Yucky Roach World

http://yucky.discovery.com/flash/roaches/
Welcome to roach world. The cool Web site for kids. You can find diary entries for a day in the life of Ralph Roach, information on roach anatomy, behavior, and life, as well as loads of gross and yucky facts.

PestWorld for Kids

www.pestworldforkids.org/cockroaches.html
This is a great site for learning about insects of all kinds. Find pictures, read infosheets, get homework help, and play games. You can also learn fun science experiments that you can do at home.

Biokids:Cockroaches

www.biokids.umich.edu/critters/Blattaria/
A great University of Michigan Web site that offers a lot of detailed information about different cockroach species.

Oggy's Fries: A Cockroach Game

www.learn4good.com/games/kids/oggys_fries.htm
Based on cartoons, this online game pits Oggy (the cat) against his three cockroach enemies, Dee Dee, Joey, and Marky. In the game, Oggy has to protect his french fries from the marauding and fast roaches.

Here are some great books on cockroaches:

Cockroaches (Creepy Creatures), by Nancy Dickman.
New York: Heinemann-Raintree, 2005.

Cockroaches, by Larry Dane Brimner.
Children's Press, 2000.

The Compleat Cockroach: A Comprehensive Guide to the Most Despised (and Least Understood) Creature on Earth
by David Gordon. Ten Speed Press, 1996.

Want to see cockroaches up close and personal? Here are some great places to visit:

American Museum of Natural History
Central Park West at 79th Street
New York, NY 10024-5192
Phone: (212) 769-5100

The Montreal Insectarium
4581 Sherbrooke East
Montréal, Québec, Canada, H1X 2B2
Phone: (514) 872-1400

Invertebrate Exhibit, The National Zoo
3001 Connecticut Ave., NW
Washington, DC 20008
Phone: (540) 635-6500

The O. Orkin Insect Zoo at the National Museum of Natural History, Smithsonian
10th Street and Constitution Ave., NW
Washington, DC 20560
Phone: (202) 633-1000

Glossary

amber The fossilized resin of a prehistoric tree that sometimes contains the remains of insects

ancestor Someone from whom a person is descended

ancestry The evolutionary or genetic line from which an animal or plant comes from

asthma A condition that makes it difficult to breathe

biologists Scientists who study living things such as plants and animals

cannibalism Eating the flesh of your own species

cardiovascular system The circulatory system of mammals such as humans that includes a heart, blood vessels, and lymph glands

circulatory system The system that circulates blood throughout a body

entomologist A scientist who studies insects

evolved To have developed certain traits over several generations

exoskeleton A rigid external covering that provides support or protection

exotic Something attractive, striking, and foreign

exterminate To destroy completely

feces Poop, or waste matter

fertile Capable of producing new plants

genetically Relating to heredity, genes, and origin

habitats The natural home or environment of an animal or plant or other living thing

Holocaust The mass murder of Jews, Gypsies, and others in Europe during the Nazi regime of World War II (1939-1945)

indestructible Not able to be destroyed

indigenous Originating or occuring naturally in a specific geographic area

infestation To be overrun with insects

invertebrates Animals lacking a backbone

microorganisms Living things, such as bacteria or fungi, that are so small they can only be seen through a microscope

originated Something that came from or began at a specific place or time

parasites Organisms that live on or in another organism, called a host

pheromones Chemical substances released by an animal that effects the behavior or function of others in its species

predators Animals that prey on others

propaganda Misleading information

radiation A form of energy which at certain levels is deadly

reproductive cycle A natural cycle where young are produced

resinous Something that is sticky

Rwandan genocide A mass slaughter of over 500,000 mostly Tutsi people by the Hutu in the African country of Rwanda in 1994

scavengers Animals that feed on dead animals or plant material

species A group of living things that have similar characteristics and are capable of interbreeding

Index